SIGHT WORDS
2nd Grade Workbook
(Baby Professor Learning Books)

ALONE

without people that you know or
that usually are with you

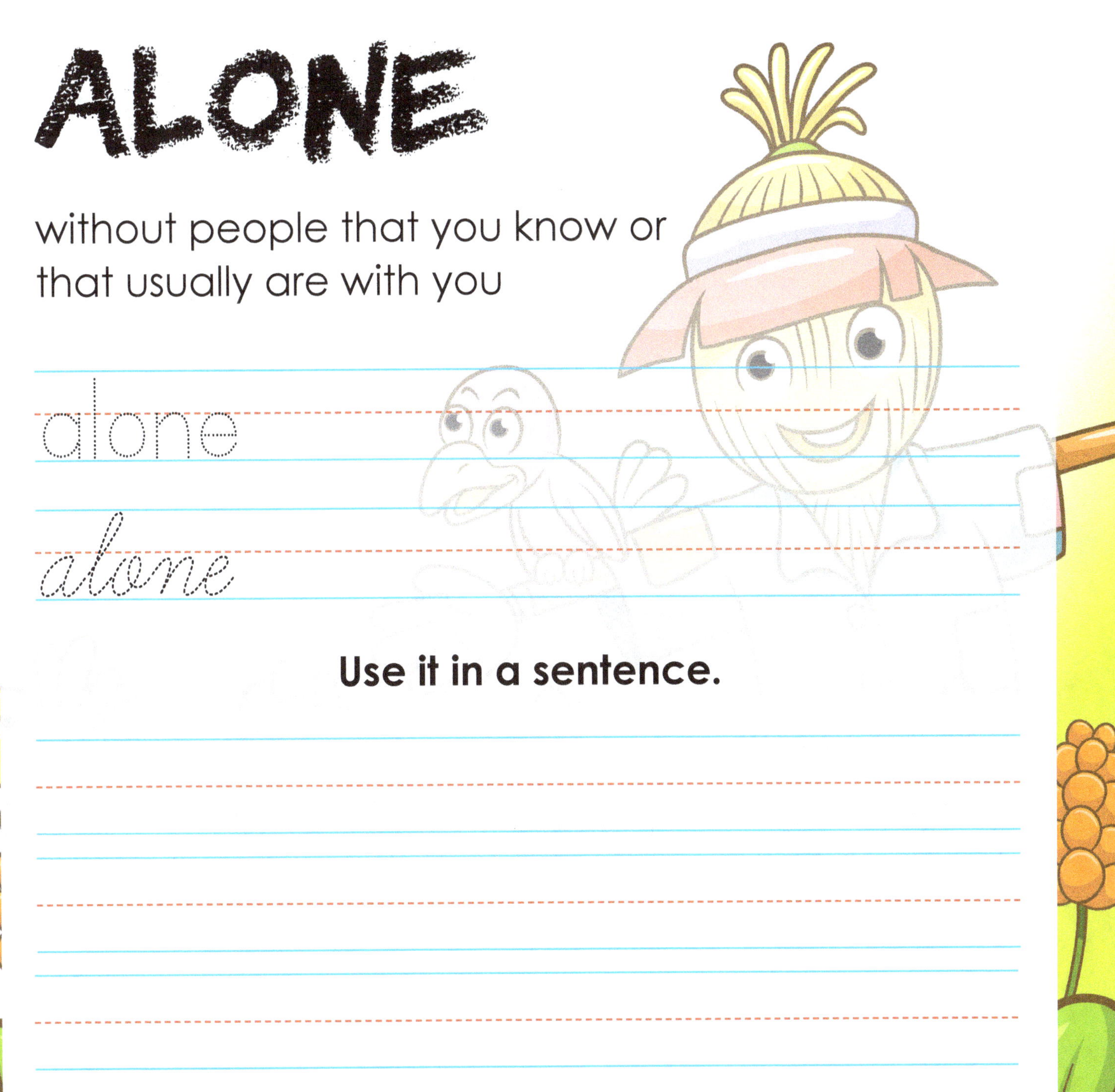

alone

alone

Use it in a sentence.

BELIEVE

to accept or regard (something) as true

believe

believe

Use it in a sentence.

BRIGHT

having a very light and strong color

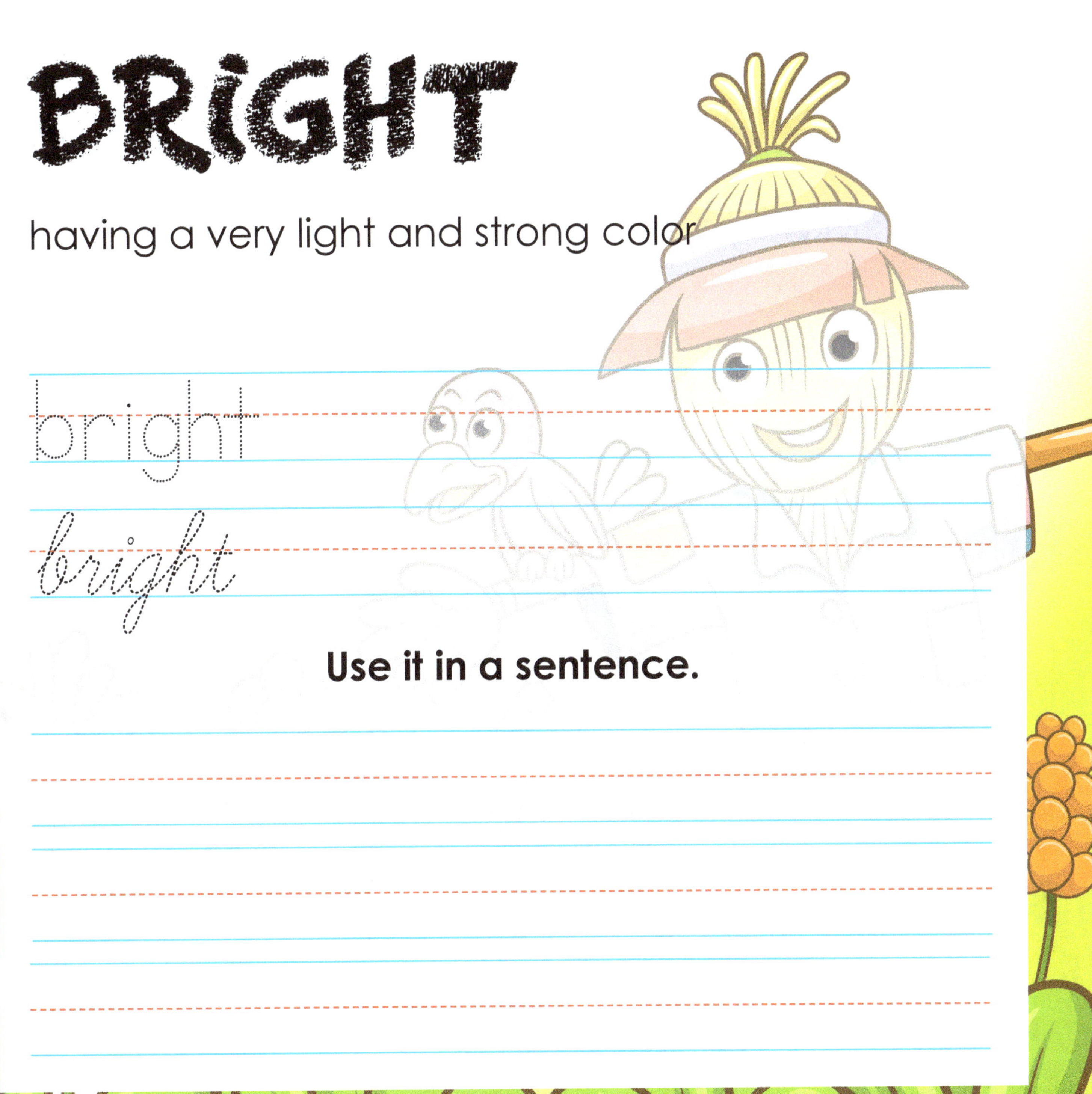

bright

bright

Use it in a sentence.

to move your body in a way that goes with the rhythm and style of music that is being played

dance

dance

Use it in a sentence.

DRIVE

to direct the movement of
(a car, truck, bus, etc.)

drive

drive

Use it in a sentence.

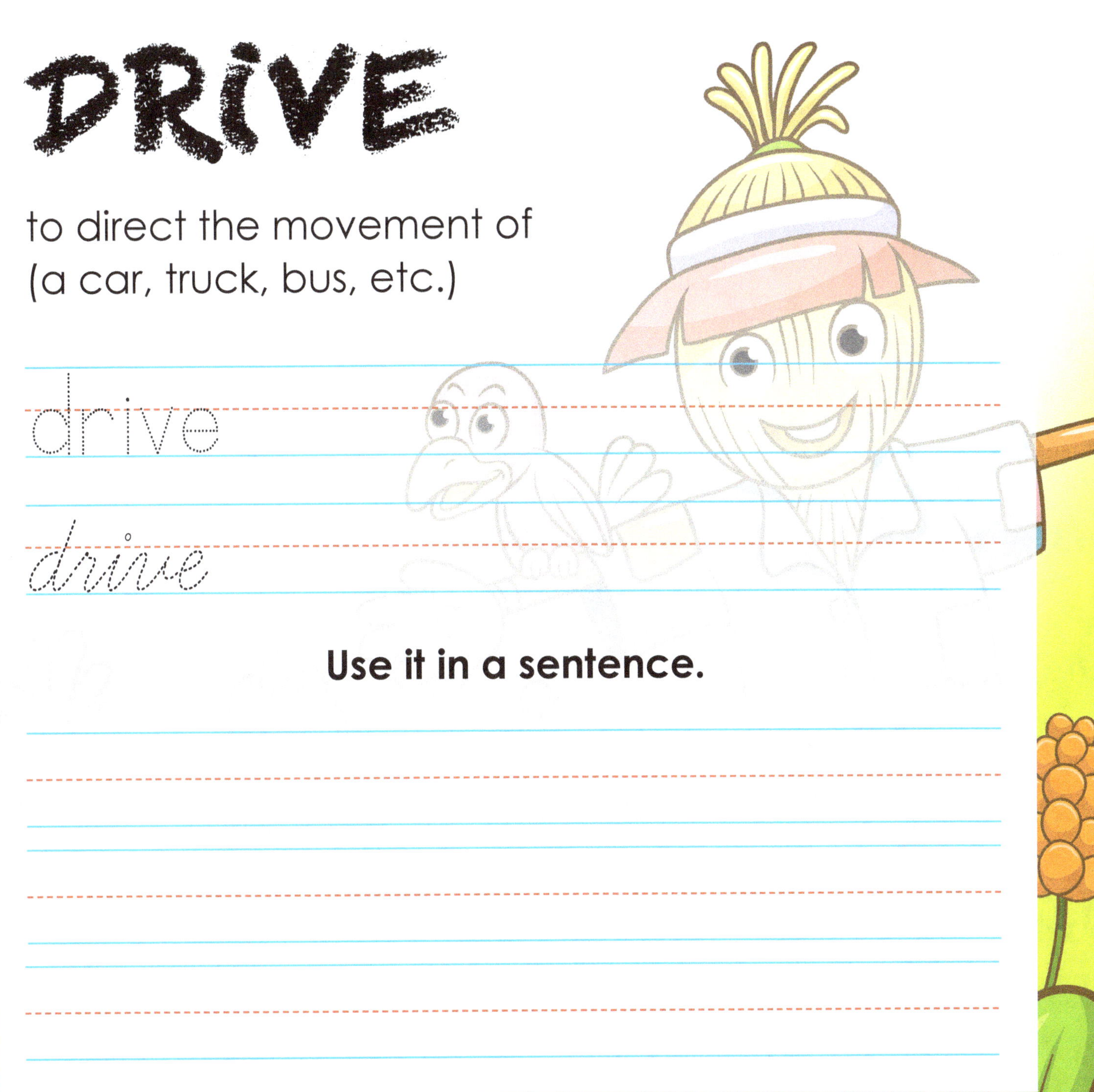

to go or come after or behind
(someone or something)

follow

follow

Use it in a sentence.

GROW

to become larger;
to increase in size, amount, etc.

grow

grow

Use it in a sentence.

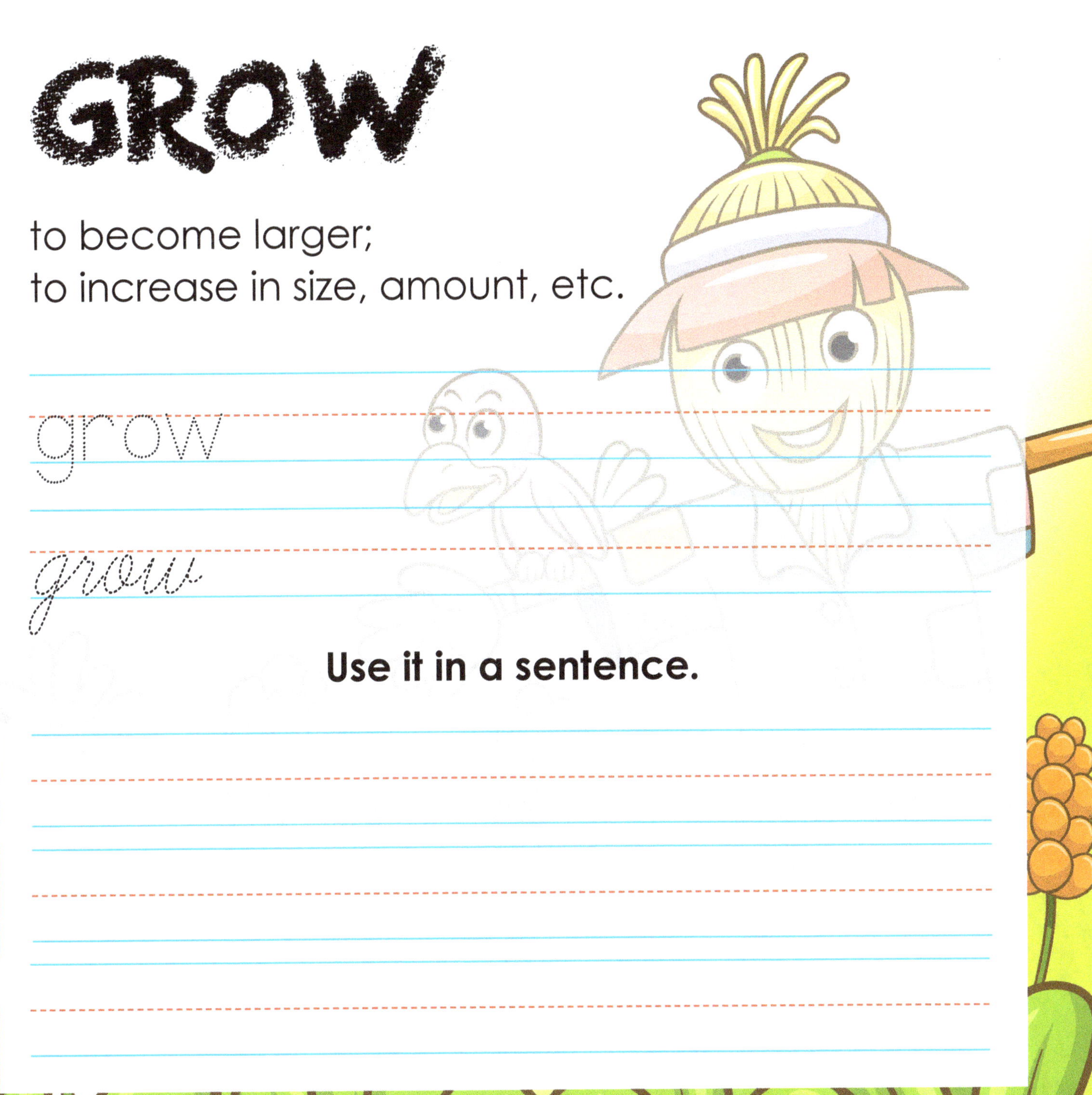

HANDLE

a part of something that is designed to be held by your hand

handle

handle

Use it in a sentence.

HURT

to cause pain or injury to (yourself, someone else, or a part of your body)

hurt

hurt

Use it in a sentence.

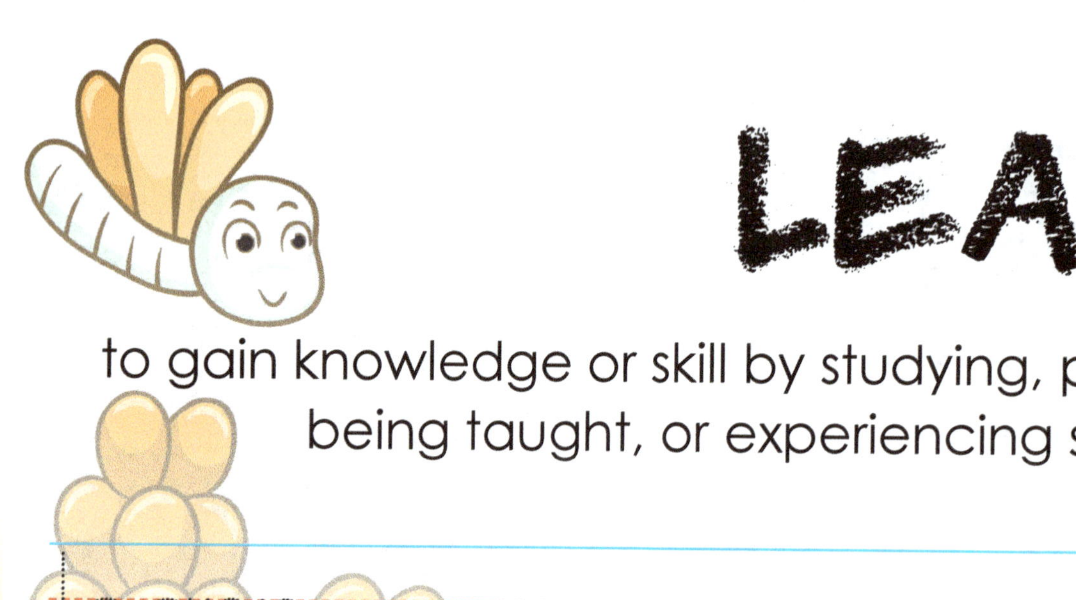

LEARN

to gain knowledge or skill by studying, practicing, being taught, or experiencing something

learn

learn

Use it in a sentence.

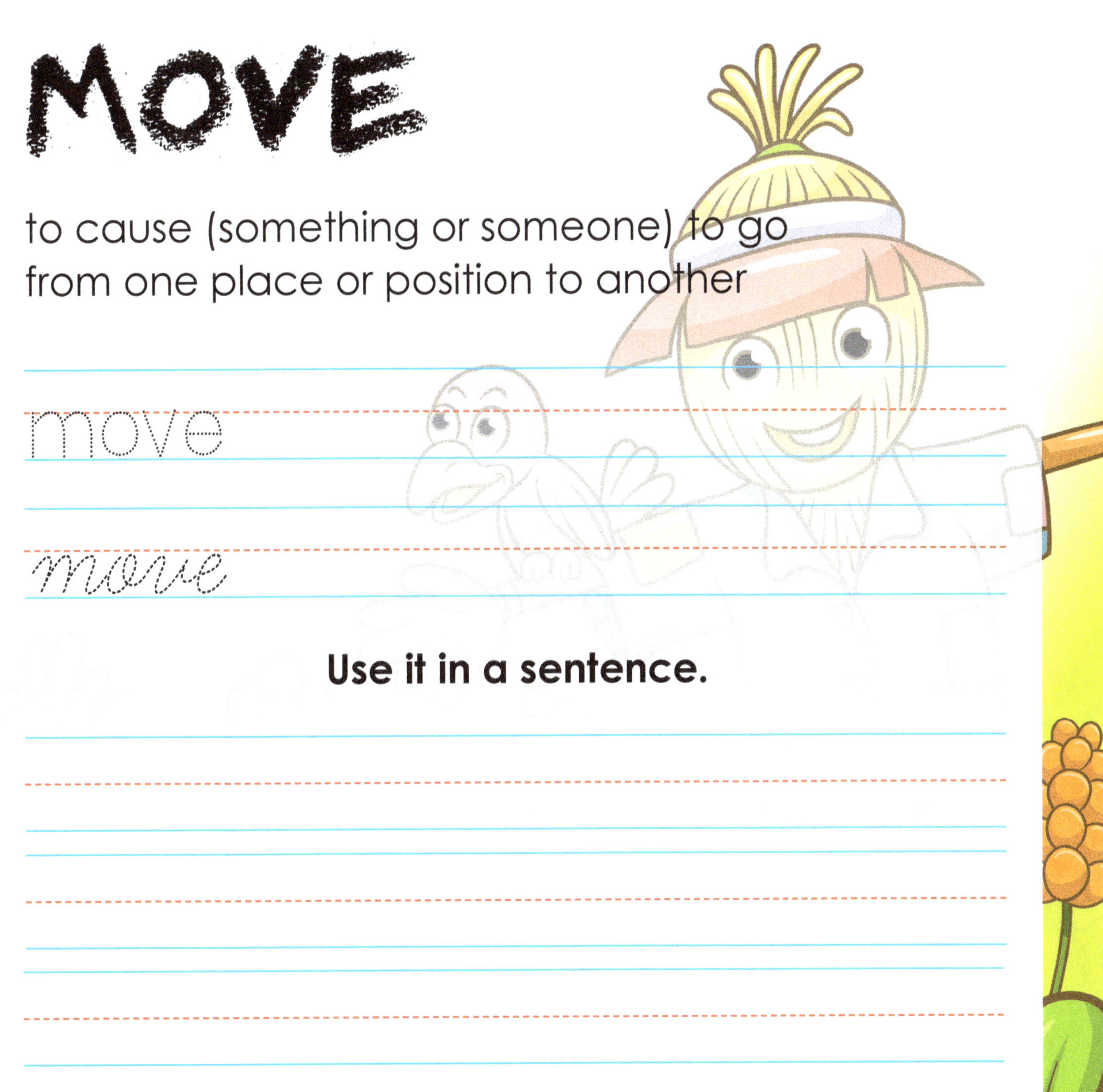

MOVE

to cause (something or someone) to go from one place or position to another

move

move

Use it in a sentence.

PUSH

to use force to move (someone or something) forward or away from you

push

push

Use it in a sentence.

REST

peace of mind or spirit

rest

rest

Use it in a sentence.

to sit on and control the movements of
(a horse, motorcycle, bicycle, etc.)

ride

ride

Use it in a sentence.

SEEN

to notice or become aware of (someone or something) by using your eyes

seen

seen

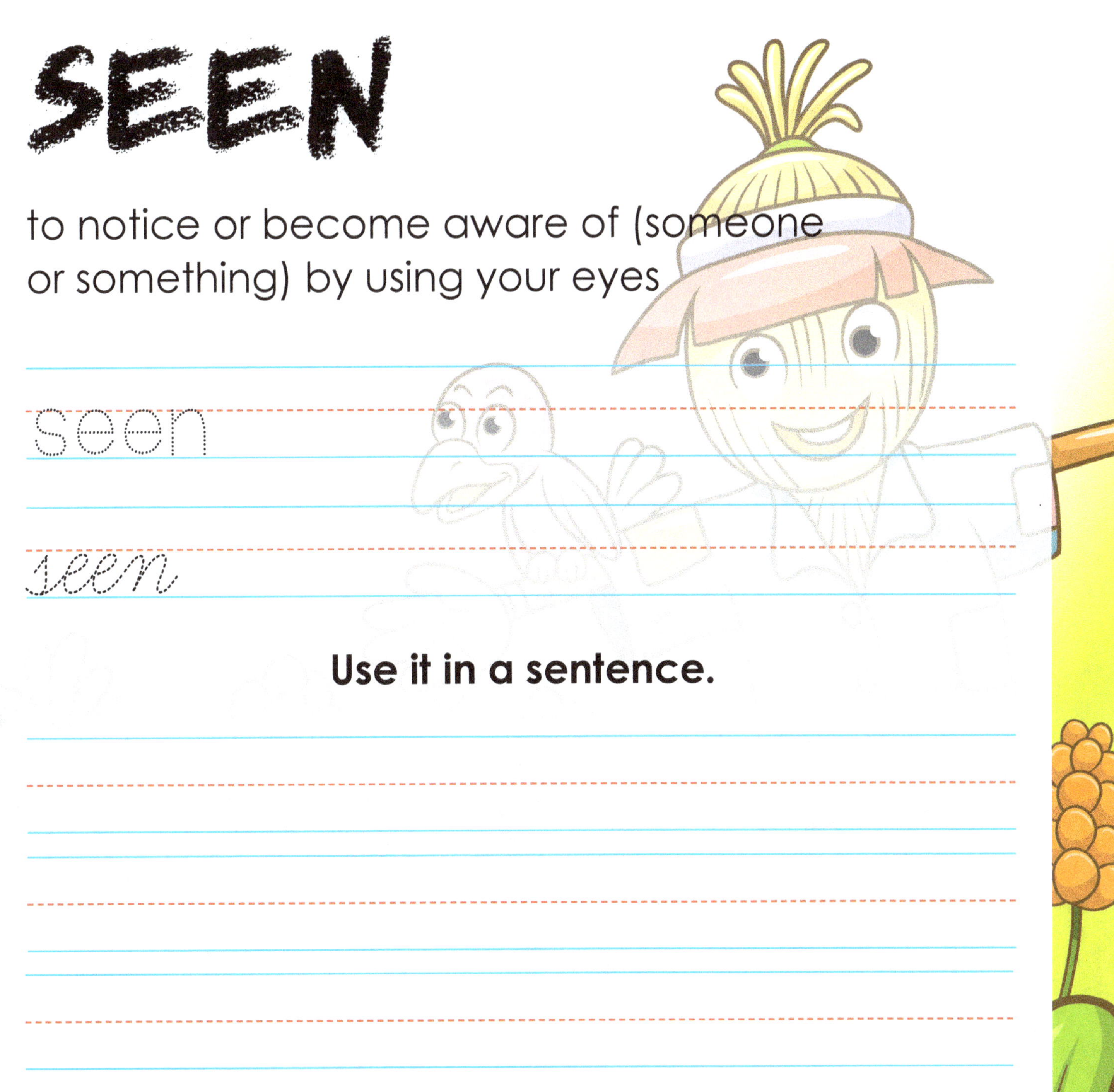

Use it in a sentence.

SHOW

to cause or allow (something) to be seen

show

show

Use it in a sentence.

SHUT

to close (something)

shut

shut

Use it in a sentence.

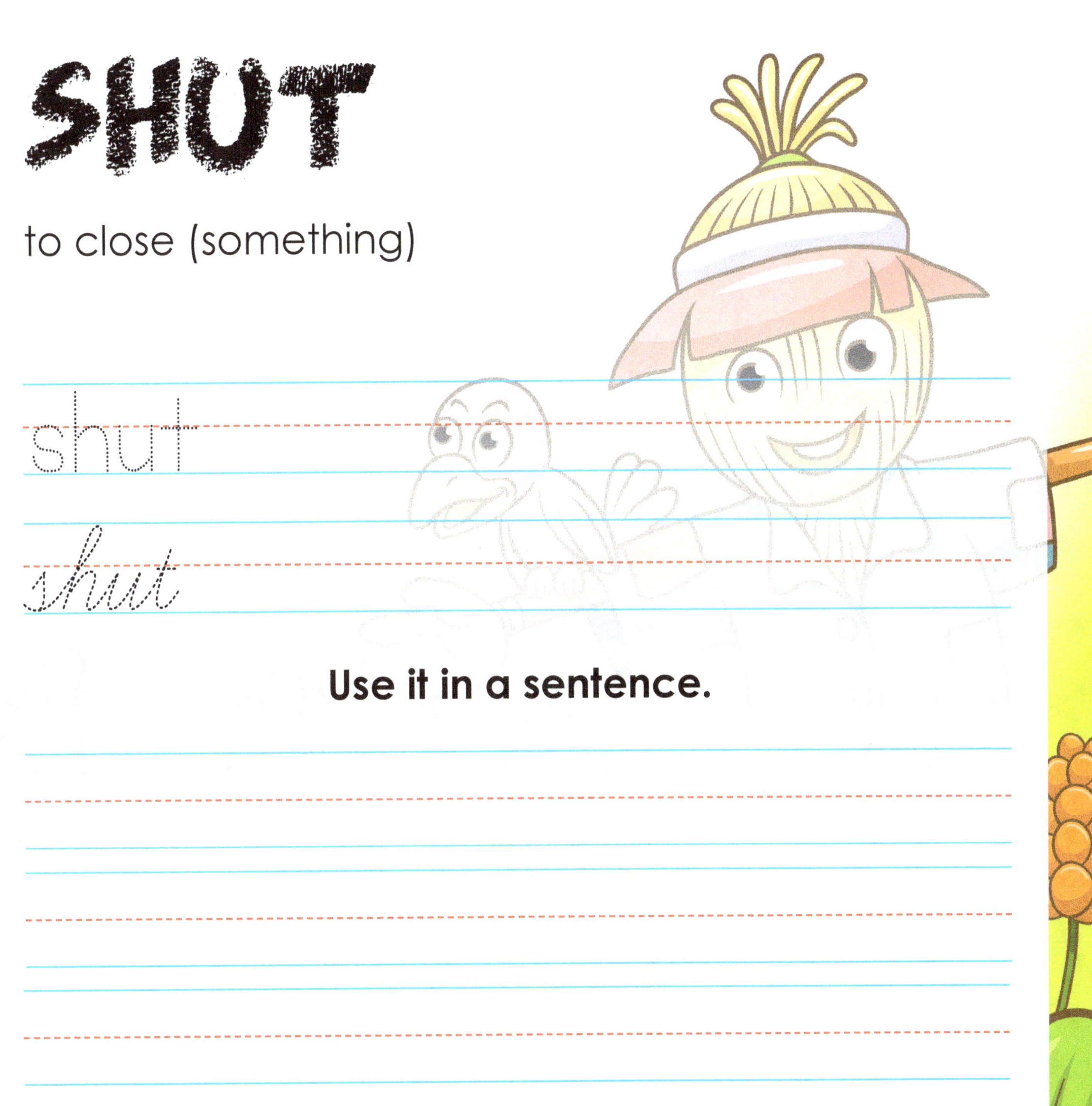

 TURN

to move around a central point

turn

turn

Use it in a sentence.

THROW

to cause (something) to move out
of your hand and through the air by
quickly moving your arm forward

throw

throw

Use it in a sentence.

to use your voice to make musical sounds in the form of a song or tune

sing

sing

Use it in a sentence.

SLED

a small vehicle that has a flat bottom or long, narrow strips of metal or wood on the bottom and that is used for moving over snow or ice

sled

sled

Use it in a sentence.

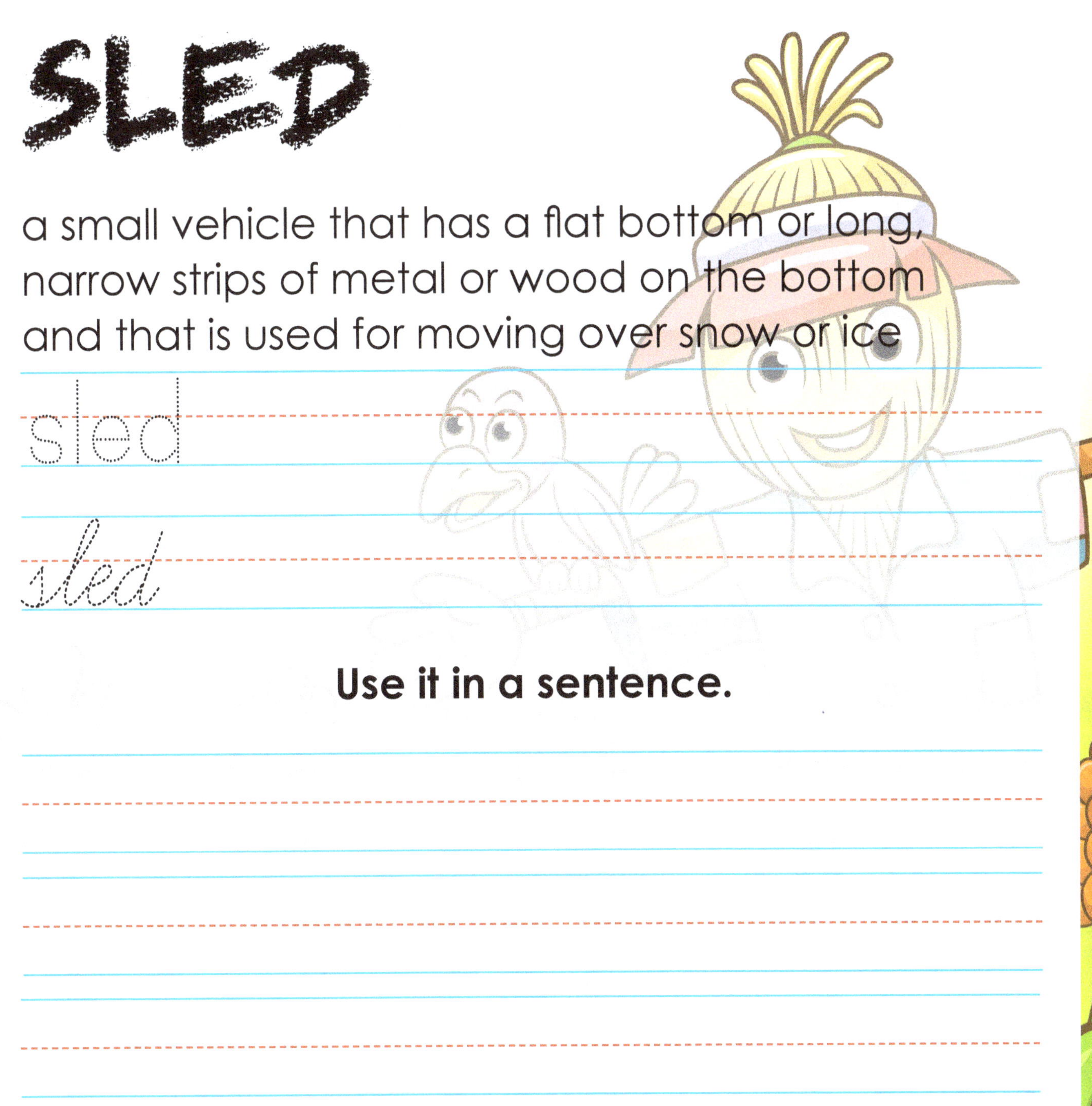

to move through water by moving
your arms and legs

swim

swim

Use it in a sentence.

THROW

to cause (something) to move out
of your hand and through the air by
quickly moving your arm forward

throw

throw

Use it in a sentence.

TRiP

to hit your foot against something while you are
walking or running so that you fall or almost fall

trip

trip

Use it in a sentence.

TRY

to make an effort to do something;
to attempt to accomplish or complete something

try

try

Use it in a sentence.

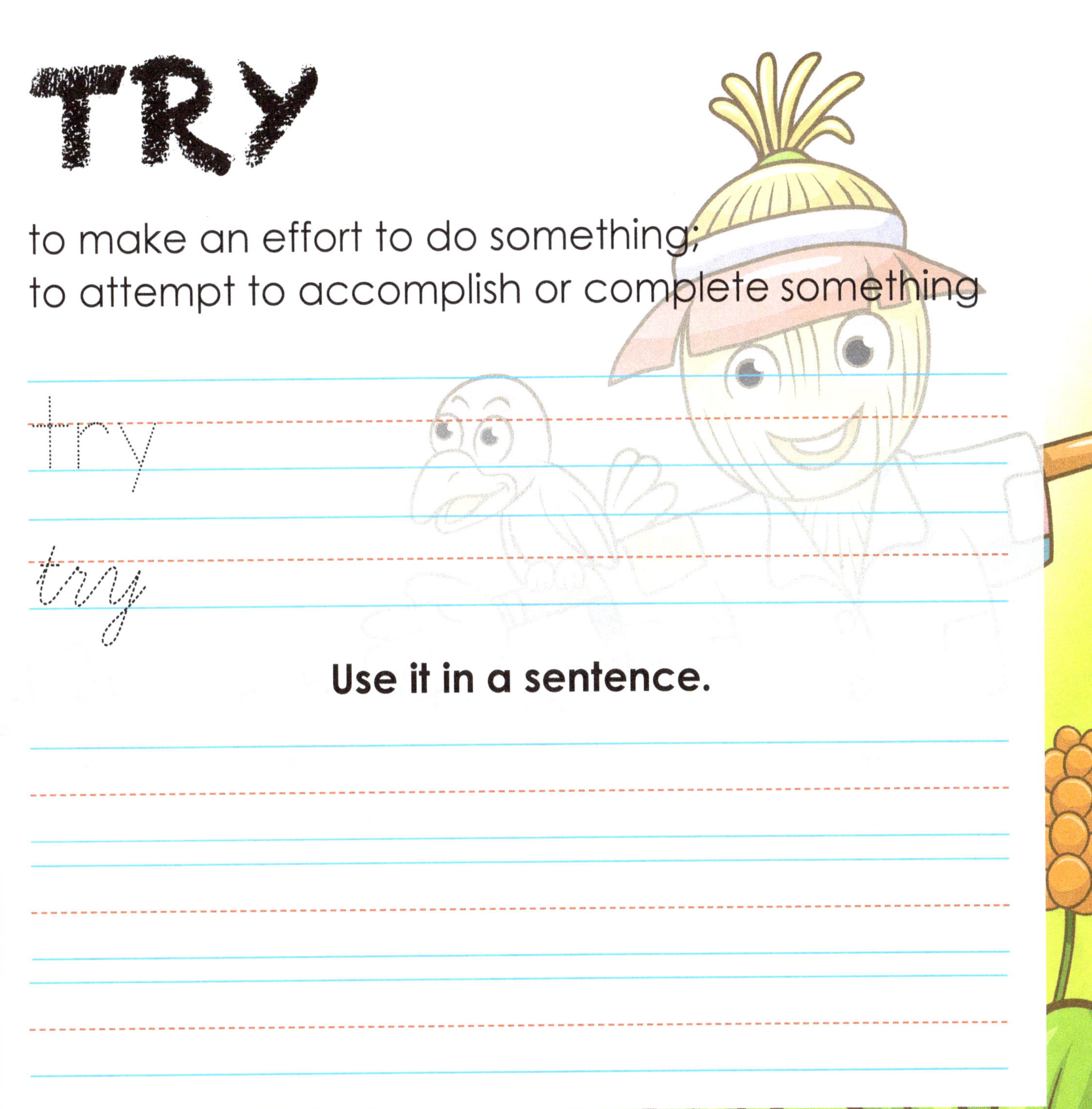

UNTIL

up to (a particular time)

until

until

Use it in a sentence.

UPON

used to say that someone or something
is very close or has arrived

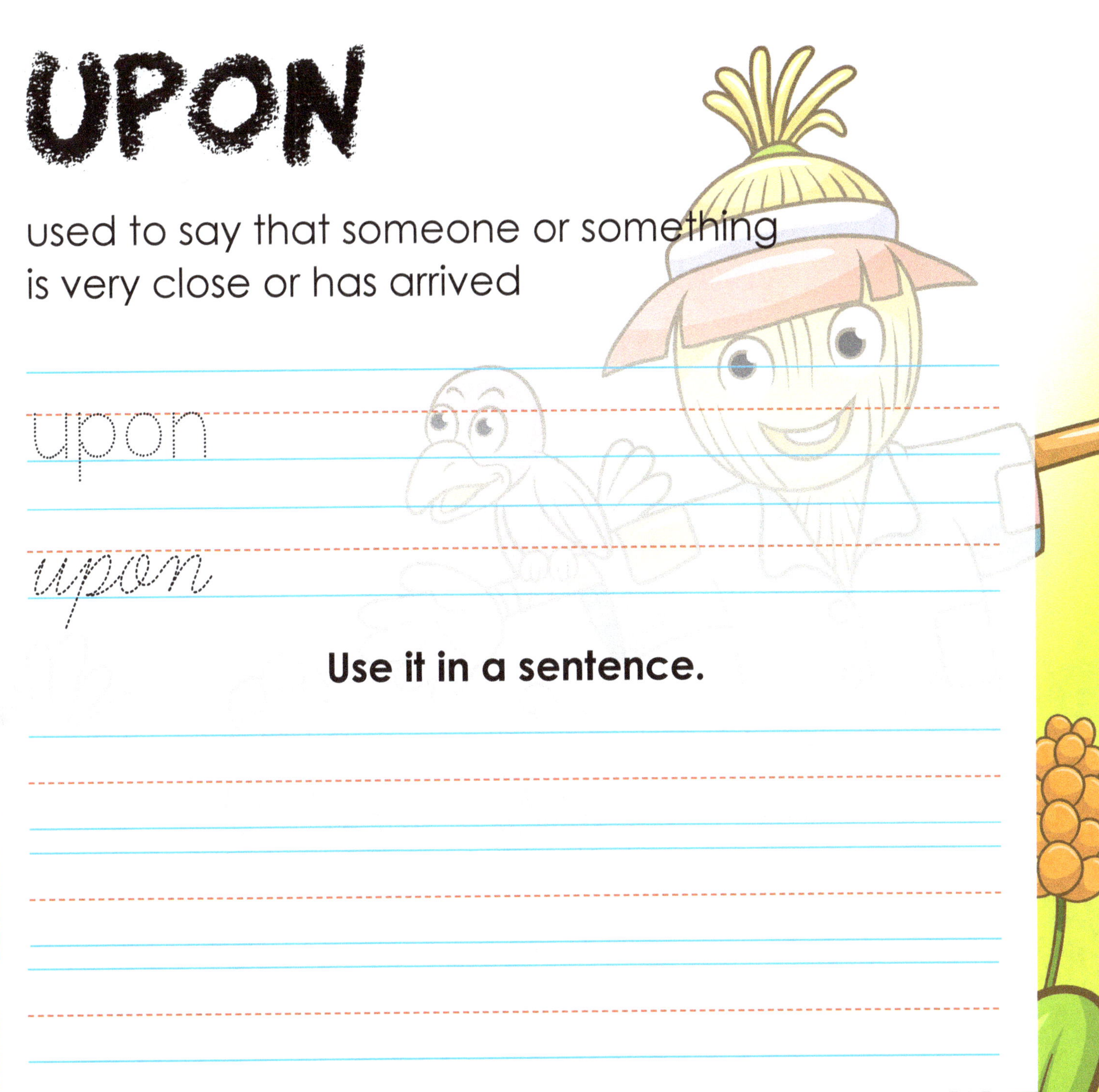

upon

upon

Use it in a sentence.

WAVE

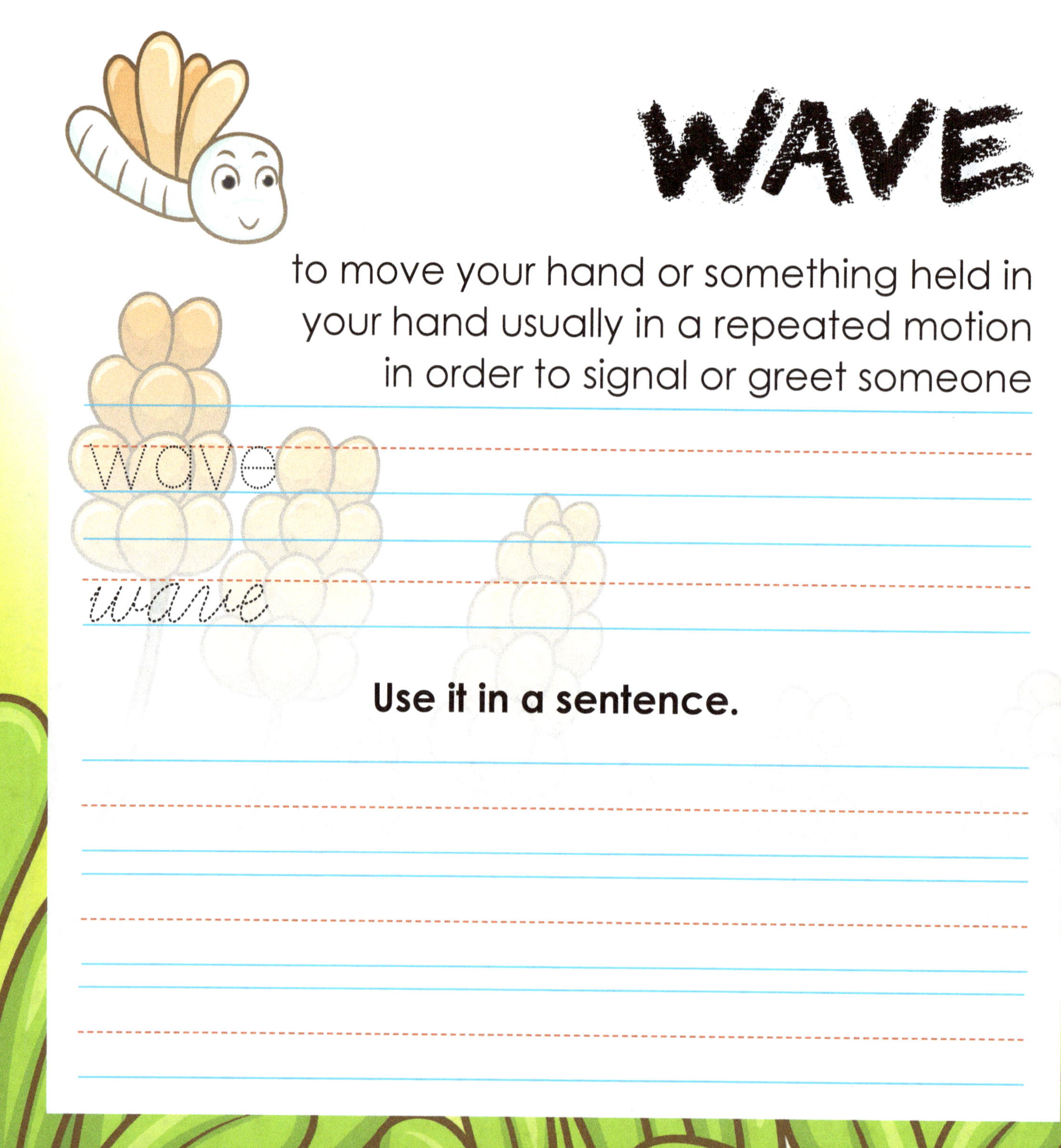

to move your hand or something held in your hand usually in a repeated motion in order to signal or greet someone

wave

wave

Use it in a sentence.

WORK

a job or activity that you do regularly especially in order to earn money

work

work

Use it in a sentence.

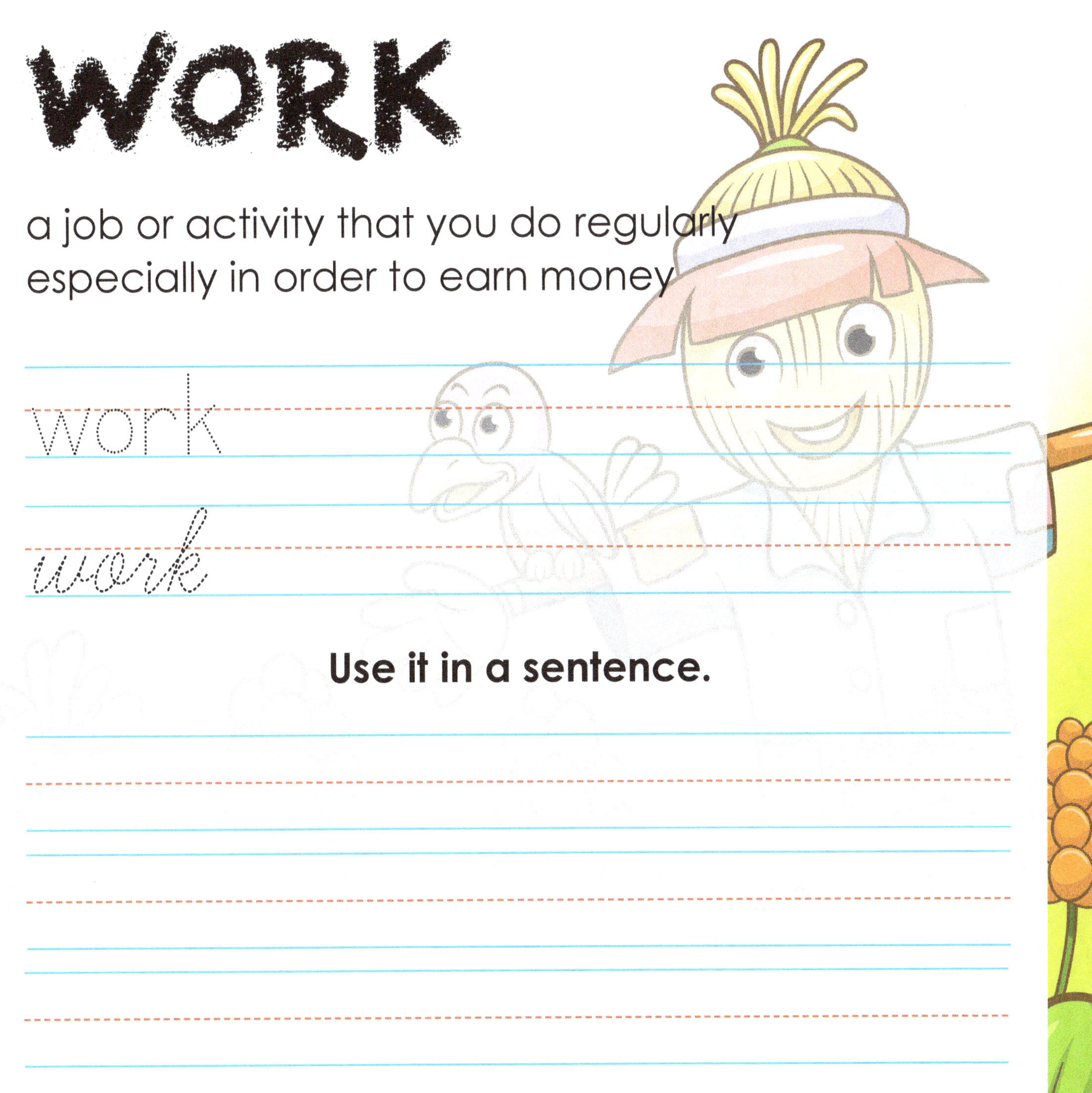

Visit
BABY PROFESSOR
EDUCATION KIDS
www.BabyProfessorBooks.com
to download Free Baby Professor eBooks
and view our catalog of new and exciting
Children's Books